SCHOLASTIC

The BIG Collection of Phonics Flipbooks

200 Reproducible Flipbooks That Target the Phonics & Word Study Skills Every Primary Student Needs to Know

Lynn Melby Gordon

NEW YORK • TORONTO • LONDON • AUCKLAND • SYDNEY
MEXICO CITY • NEW DELHI • HONG KONG • BUENOS AIRES

Teaching *Resources*

Teachers,

You are to be commended for holding high the torch of literacy and lighting the way for each of your students. As you know, when you teach a child to read, you open an exciting door and change his or her life forever. Thus, teaching is a truly noble endeavor. Go forth to teach with enthusiasm! May you experience the delight of watching the doors open and watching the light of literacy spread as your students sprint forward to embrace a lifetime of reading, learning, and pleasure.

Lynn Melby Gordon, Ph.D.
Department of Elementary Education
California State University, Northridge

Teachers who wish to contact Dr. Gordon may visit her Web site at phonics.info.

Cover design by Brian LaRossa
Interior design by Solas
Pages 19–240 based on designs by Lynn Melby Gordon

ISBN-13: 978-0-545-07418-6
ISBN-10: 0-545-07418-5

Copyright © 2009 by Lynn Melby Gordon
Published by Scholastic Inc.
All rights reserved.
Printed in the U.S.A.

1 2 3 4 5 6 7 8 9 10   40   16 15 14 13 12 11 10 09

Contents

Short *u*

70	-ub	cub, hub, rub, sub, tub, club, scrub
71	-ud	bud, cud, dud, mud, crud, spud, thud
72	-uck	duck, luck, puck, suck, tuck, stuck, truck
73	-uff	buff, cuff, huff, puff, fluff, scuff, stuff
74	-ug	bug, dug, hug, jug, mug, rug, tug
75	-um	gum, hum, rum, sum, chum, drum, plum
76	-ump	bump, dump, hump, jump, lump, pump, thump
77	-un	bun, fun, gun, pun, run, sun, spun
78	-unch	bunch, lunch, munch, punch, brunch, crunch, scrunch
79	-ung	hung, lung, sung, clung, slung, sprung, strung
80	-unk	bunk, hunk, junk, sunk, drunk, skunk, trunk
81	-unt	bunt, hunt, punt, runt, blunt, grunt, stunt
82	-ush	hush, mush, rush, blush, brush crush, flush
83	-ust	dust, gust, just, must, rust, crust, trust
84	-ut	but, cut, gut, hut, nut, rut, shut

Long Vowels With Silent *e*

Long *a*

85	-ace	ace, face, lace, race, brace, place, space, trace
86	-ade	fade, made, wade, blade, grade, shade, trade
87	-age	age, cage, page, rage, sage, wage, stage
88	-ake	bake, cake, lake, make, take, wake, snake
89	-ale	ale, male, pale, sale, tale, scale, stale, whale
90	-ame	came, game, name, same, blame, flame, frame
91	-ane	cane, Jane, lane, mane, pane, crane, plane
92	-ape	ape, cape, gape, tape, drape, grape, scrape, shape
93	-ate	ate, date, gate, hate, late, plate, skate, state
94	-ave	cave, Dave, gave, save, wave, brave, grave
95	-aze	daze, gaze, haze, maze, blaze, craze, glaze

Long *i*

96	-ice	ice, dice, mice, nice, rice, price, slice, twice
97	-ide	hide, ride, side, wide, bride, glide, slide
98	-ife	fife, life, rife, wife, strife
99	-ike	bike, hike, like, Mike, spike, strike, trike
100	-ile	file, mile, pile, tile, vile, smile, while
101	-ime	dime, lime, time, chime, crime, grime, slime
102	-ine	dine, fine, line, mine, nine, pine, vine
103	-ipe	pipe, ripe, wipe, gripe, snipe, swipe, stripe
104	-ite	bite, kite, mite, site, quite, spite, white
105	-ive	dive, five, hive, jive, live, drive, strive

Long *o*

106	-oke	joke, poke, woke, broke, choke, smoke, spoke
107	-ole	dole, hole, mole, pole, role, sole, stole
108	-one	bone, cone, zone, clone, phone, shone, stone
109	-ope	cope, dope, hope, mope, nope, grope, scope
110	-ose	hose, nose, pose, rose, chose, close, those
111	-ote	dote, note, rote, tote, vote, quote
112	-ove	cove, wove, clove, drove, grove, stove, trove

Long *u*

113	-ude	dude, nude, rude, crude, prude
114	-ute	cute, jute, lute, mute, brute, flute

Other Long Vowel Phonograms

115	-ail	ail, fail, jail, mail, nail, pail, sail, snail
116	-ain	main, pain, rain, brain, plain, stain, train
117	-ay	day, may, pay, say, way, gray, play
118	-e	be, he, me, we, she
119	-ea	pea, sea, tea, flea, plea
120	-each	each, beach, leach, peach, reach, teach, bleach, preach
121	-eak	beak, leak, peak, weak, sneak, speak, squeak
122	-eal	deal, heal, meal, real, seal, steal, squeal
123	-eam	beam, team, cream, dream, steam, scream, stream
124	-eat	eat, beat, heat, meat, neat, seat, bleat, cheat

125 -ee   bee, fee, see, flee, free, tree, three

126 -eed   feed, need, seed, weed, bleed, greed, speed

127 -eek   peek, seek, week, cheek, creek, Greek, sleek

128 -eel   eel, feel, heel, keel, peel, reel, steel, wheel

129 -eep   beep, deep, jeep, keep, weep, cheep, sleep

130 -eet   beet, feet, meet, greet, sheet, sweet, street

131 -ight   fight, light, might, right, sight, tight, bright

132 -ind   bind, find, kind, mind, wind, blind, grind

133 -oat   oat, boat, coat, goat, moat, float, gloat, throat

134 -old   old, cold, fold, gold, hold, mold, sold, told

135 -ow   low, mow, crow, grow, show, snow

136 -own   own, mown, blown, flown, grown, shown, thrown

137 -y   by, my, cry, fly, sky, try, shy, why

Diphthongs

138 -oil   oil, boil, coil, foil, soil, toil, broil, spoil

139 -ouch   ouch, couch, pouch, vouch, crouch, grouch, slouch

140 -ound   bound, found, hound, pound, round, sound, ground

141 -ouse   house, louse, mouse, blouse, grouse, spouse

142 -out   out, pout, scout, shout, spout, trout, sprout

143 -ow   ow, cow, how, now, vow, wow, brow, plow

144 -owl   owl, fowl, howl, jowl, growl, prowl, scowl

145 -own   down, town, brown, clown, crown, drown, frown

146 -oy   boy, coy, joy, Roy, soy, toy, ploy

Variant Vowel Phonograms

147 -all   all, call, fall, mall, tall, wall, small, stall

148 -aw   aw, jaw, law, paw, raw, saw, draw, straw

149 -awn   dawn, fawn, lawn, pawn, yawn, drawn, prawn

150 -ew   dew, new, blew, chew, crew, threw

151 -ong   gong, long, song, tong, prong, strong

152 -oo   boo, coo, goo, moo, too, zoo

153 -ook   book, cook, hook, look, took, brook, shook

154 -ool   cool, fool, pool, tool, drool, school, stool

155 -oom   boom, room, zoom, bloom, broom, gloom, groom

156 -oop   coop, hoop, loop, droop, scoop, snoop, troop

157 -oot   boot, hoot, loot, root, toot, scoot, shoot

158 -oss   boss, loss, moss, toss, cross, floss, gloss

R-Controlled Vowels

159 -air   air, fair, hair, pair, chair, flair, stair

160 -ar   bar, car, far, jar, tar, scar, star

161 -are   bare, care, rare, scare, share, stare, square

162 -ark   bark, dark, mark, park, Clark, shark, spark

163 -art   cart, dart, part, tart, chart, smart, start

164 -ear   ear, dear, fear, gear, hear, year, clear, smear

165 -irt   dirt, flirt, shirt, skirt, squirt

166 -ore   ore, more, sore, wore, chore, score, snore, store

167 -ork   cork, fork, pork, York, stork

168 -orn   born, corn, horn, torn, worn, scorn, thorn

169 -ort   fort, Mort, port, sort, short, snort, sport

Initial Consonant Blends

170 bl-   bled, blob, black, blast, blend, blond, blush

171 br-   brad, bran, brat, brim, brand, brass, brick

172 cl-   clam, clap, clip, club, class, cliff, clock

173 cr-   crab, crib, crop, crack, craft, cross, crust

174 dr-   drag, drip, drop, drug, drum, dress, drill

175 fl-   flag, flat, flip, flop, flock, floss, fluff

176 fr-   fret, frog, fresh, frill, frizz, frost, free

177 gl-   glad, glop, glum, gland, glass, glint, gloss

178 gr-   grab, grin, grip, grit, grub, grant, grass

179 pl-   plan, plop, plot, plug, plum, plus, plant

180 pr-   prim, prod, prop, press, prick, primp, print

181 qu-   quit, quiz, quack, quest, quick, quill, quilt

182 sc-   scab, scan, scam, scat, scum, scoff, scuff

183 scr-   scrap, scrub, scratch, scrape, scream, screen

184	sk-	skid, skin, skip, skit, skill, skull, skunk
185	sl-	slam, slap, slid, slip, slug, slant, slept
186	sm-	smug, smack, smash, smell, smelt, smock
187	sn-	snap, snip, snob, snub, snug, snack, sniff
188	squ-	squid, squint, squish, squeak, squeal, squeeze, square
189	sp-	spin, spit, spot, spell, spend, spent, spill
190	spl-	splat, split, splash, splint, splosh, splotch
191	st-	step, stop, stamp, stand, stick, stiff, still
192	str-	strap, strip, stress, string, strong, struck, street
193	sw-	swam, swim, swell, swept, swing, swish, switch
194	tr-	trap, trim, trip, trot, track, truck, trust
195	tw-	twig, twin, twitch, twice, twine, tweed, tweet

Initial Consonant Digraphs

196	ch-	chat, chin, chop, check, chest, chick, chill
197	sh-	shin, ship, shop, shut, shack, shell, shock
198	th-	than, that, them, then, this, these, those
199	th-	thin, thud, thank, thick, think, thing, thump
200	thr-	throb, thrash, thrill, thrush, three, throat, throw
201	wh-	why, when, whip, which, whale, white, wheel

PREFIXES & SUFFIXES
Prefixes

202	dis-	disobey, dislike, disagree, discover, disinfect, displace
203	pre-	prepay, precook, pretest, preview, premature, preschool
204	re-	redo, react, refill, remove, return, replay
205	sub-	submarine, subdivide, subtest, suburban, subway
206	un-	unzip, unkind, unlock, uncover, unhappy, unlucky

Suffixes

207	-ed /d/	called, fizzed, pulled, yelled, mailed, spilled, stormed
208	-ed /t/	mixed, cooked, kicked, kissed, helped, fished, wished
209	-ed /ed/	dented, landed, listed, melted, needed, tested, planted
210	-er	golfer, helper, painter, pitcher, singer, teacher
211	-ful	careful, helpful, hopeful, painful, playful, respectful
212	-ing	doing, acting, saying, calling, looking, telling, spelling
213	-less	jobless, fearless, helpless, homeless, hopeless, sleepless
214	-ly	gladly, neatly, rudely, safely, softly, quietly
215	-ment	shipment, payment, treatment, agreement, excitement, punishment
216	-s /s/	cats, cuts, hops, lips, naps, pets, zips
217	-s /z/	bags, beds, bugs, cans, kids, hogs, hugs
218	-y	dirty, dusty, sandy, brainy, glassy, frosty, sleepy

DICTATION & ASSESSMENTS
Dictation

Assessments

INTRODUCTION

Welcome to *The Big Collection of Phonics Flipbooks*! The 200 reproducible flipbooks and 20 phonics assessments in this book target essential phonics skills such as basic blending, onsets, rimes, prefixes, and suffixes. These materials are designed to inspire engaged learning and provide students with multi-sensory, hands-on, phonetic reading practice. As beginning and early readers construct and use the flipbooks, they get important practice in sound blending, building words, and decoding helpful phonograms, such as *–at* (*at, bat, cat, fat, mat, pat, rat, sat*) and *–ing* (*king, ring, sing, wing, bring, thing, swing*).

In this comprehensive collection, you will find a phonics flipbook for almost every word family that has at least six or seven related words. Flipbooks are also provided for initial consonant blends and digraphs, as well as common prefixes and suffixes. No matter what grade level or reading series you use with students, you will find appropriate flipbooks to supplement your phonics lessons. In addition, you can use the reproducible dictation page and phonics skill tests to monitor student progress, assess mastery, communicate with parents, and identify lesson objectives. Information about phonics and reading research, important teaching tips, and useful word lists for phonics and spelling instruction are also included in this resource.

The materials in *The Big Collection of Phonics Flipbooks* are great for use with beginning readers of all ages, English learners, struggling readers, students in intervention programs, adult learners, and students with learning disabilities, visual impairment, or dyslexia. The activities are designed for use with your reading curriculum as a way to highlight and review important phonics skills, interject variety, and motivate reluctant learners. This collection, which has been successfully piloted with students in the Los Angeles area, supports national and regional mandates for the inclusion of systematic and explicit phonics instruction in beginning reading instruction programs. It also provides practical activities and assessments that teachers can use to address state and district standards for phonics skill mastery.

About the Author

Dr. Lynn Melby Gordon is a full-time tenured professor in the Department of Elementary Education at California State University, Northridge where she specializes in teacher education, reading methodology, and English language development. She taught elementary school for fourteen years, was an LAUSD mentor teacher, and frequently served as a supervising teacher for CSUN and UCLA student teachers. Dr. Gordon holds a Ph.D. in Education from UCLA and is the founder of the International Reading Association's Phonics Special Interest Group.

ABOUT PHONICS INSTRUCTION

What is Phonics?

Phonics is a method of beginning reading instruction that focuses on teaching students the sounds of the letters, the sounds of spelling patterns, and oral blending. Our alphabetic writing system is fundamentally a code system, with the letters and letter combinations standing for spoken sounds. Learning to read words involves decoding or breaking the code and translating the printed symbols back into speech, at first orally and, later, silently. For example, when kindergartners are taught that *h* says /h/ as in *house*, that *a* says /a/ as in *apple* and that *t* says /t/ as in *tiger*—and are then prompted to blend the sounds /h/-/a/-/t/ together to read *hat*—they are learning to read with phonics.

Effective phonics instruction provides clear, explicit, and carefully sequenced lessons that proceed from simple letter-sound associations to more complex spelling pattern-sound associations. Teachers should model careful sound blending for students and provide ample, deliberate oral word reading and writing practice. The use of these strategies helps beginning readers accurately decode, recall sounds, blend sounds into words, and cement the phonetic reading skill set into a dominant and highly efficient cognitive habit.

To maximize success, most phonics-based beginning reading programs are designed to give students practice in reading with specially designed "decodables"—easy sentences and short stories often in little-book form and containing a high percentage of phonetically sound-out-able words composed of previously taught sounds and patterns. Although critics sometimes scoff at decodable text, especially densely rhymed sentences such as "Nan ran to the tan van," well-written decodable text gives students the support they need to move from basic phonics and word blending to reading sentences and short stories. It also serves as a safe, comfortable stepping stone as students proceed down the path to reading more difficult literature.

Why Teach Phonics?

Since the early 1990's, the inclusion of systematic and explicit phonics instruction for beginning and struggling readers has become the focus of an important reading reform and school improvement movement across the United States and in many other English-speaking countries. This is largely due to the dissemination of influential and comprehensive reading research reports such as *Beginning to Read: Thinking and Learning About Print* by Marilyn Adams, *Preventing Reading Difficulties in Young Children*, edited by Snow, Burns, and Griffin, and *The Report of the National Reading Panel: Teaching Children to Read*. After reviewing countless empirical studies, researchers found that phonics instruction aids reading at the word level. Furthermore, it produces a cascade of benefits including improved fluency, spelling, and, to some extent, comprehension.

In 2001, the No Child Left Behind (NCLB) legislation required states and districts in the United States to fund only evidence-based reading programs. In response, phonics was officially put back in the curriculum and the law has been widely credited with raising reading achievement across the nation. In addition, state and national reading organizations updated their standards to clarify the importance of phonics and emphasize the urgency of embracing scientifically based reading instruction. The following research shows a variety of positive outcomes associated with instruction in phonemic awareness (the ability to differentiate and manipulate the individual spoken sounds in words) and phonics.

- Phonemic awareness allows students to benefit from phonics instruction and predicts reading achievement (Adams, 2000; Shaywitz, 2003).

- Phonemic awareness training normalizes brain function in dyslexics and improves reading ability (Shaywitz, 2003; Temple, 2003).

- Phonemic awareness training is more effective when it is taught with letters (National Reading Panel, 2000).

- Systematic phonics instruction produces significant benefits for students in kindergarten through 6th grade (National Reading Panel).

- Systematic phonics instruction produces significant benefits for struggling readers as well as for students with learning disabilities (National Reading Panel).

- Systematic synthetic phonics instruction is significantly more effective in improving low socioeconomic status (SES) than instructional approaches that are less focused on these initial reading skills (National Reading Panel).

- Phonics instruction is associated with significant improvement in students' ability to comprehend text. (National Reading Panel).

- Across all grade levels, systematic phonics instruction improves the ability of good readers to spell (National Reading Panel).

- Explicit phonics instruction helps English learners acquire English reading skills (equivalent to native speakers) in two to three years (Resnick, 2004).

- Systematic and strategic rime-based and phoneme-based phonics instruction is associated with improved word reading (White, 2005; Wylie & Durell, 1970) and reading comprehension (White, 2005).

Teaching Tip

Use lowercase letters for phonics instruction. Many beginning and struggling readers are familiar only with the shapes of the capital letters. Teach students to automatically recognize the lowercase letters (and the sounds associated with those letters) before using the phonics flipbooks.

How Do I Begin Teaching Phonics?

When preparing for phonics instruction, plan to teach the basic (most frequent) letter sounds before asking students to read words. You can use the Letter-Sound Chart on page 17 as a guide to teach the individual sound for each letter of the alphabet. A good rule of thumb, at the preschool and kindergarten level, is to spend at least two days to a week on each letter and sound.

Effective letter-sound instruction is vivid, engaging, multisensory, and often involves the use of puppets, songs, alliterative chants, kinesthetic memory cues (pantomimed actions to go along with and reinforce the sound being taught), and, especially, objects or picture cards that begin with the featured sound. Plan an array of motivating activities and hands-on projects to help anchor the primary sound for each letter in students' memories. As you focus on each letter-sound correspondence, display the letter in large print—using its lowercase form—on half-sheets of tagboard or construction paper to help reinforce the association of its sound with the printed letter. (Capital letters are much less important since readers encounter them in text less frequently.)

Are Short Vowels Sounds Important?

Yes! Students who do not know their short vowel sounds often fail to learn how to blend small words sound by sound—a crucial first step in learning how to read. When students begin to practice blending sounds and reading words, present them with numerous three-letter consonant-vowel-consonant (CVC) words, such as *cat, hen, win, fog,* and *sun.* Help them understand that when a vowel is between two consonants, such as in these words, it very reliably makes its short vowel sound. Students must learn the short vowel sounds to the point of mastery to enable successful early blending practice with CVC words. When referring to the vowel sounds during instruction, be careful to say the actual sounds and not the letter names.

Is it improper to say that a letter "says" or "makes" a certain sound?

While literacy experts are not in full agreement, the answer to this question is basically "No." Perhaps, because young children learn that cats say "Meow," and cows say "Moo," it makes sense to them when a teacher explains that "*S* says /s/" or "*S* makes the /s/ sound like we hear at the beginning of *s-s-snake.*" Children accept and process this direct and commonsensical explanation easily and the use of these terms can be a good, clear way to help students understand the link between spoken and written language. Letters and letter combinations are the written symbols of our speech, and when we read, we actually are translating the symbols into sounds, in our minds, if not aloud.

ABOUT THIS BOOK

What's Inside?

Here's what you'll find in *The Big Collection of Phonics Flipbooks*:

- 200 Reproducible Phonics Flipbooks—Easy-to-assemble flipbooks are designed to give students phonetic reading practice in basic blending, onsets, rimes, prefixes, and suffixes. The word strip at the top of each reproducible page lists the words featured in the flipbook and can also be used to reinforce learning (see Extension Activities on page 15).

- Phonics Dictation Recording Sheet—Students practice sound-spelling relationships by writing dictated words on copies of this reproducible.

- Assessments—The results from The Alphabet Sounds Test and Phonics Skill Tests can be used to guide your phonics instruction, evaluate and track individual learning, and communicate student progress with families.

How Are the Flipbooks Constructed?

Making each phonics flipbook is easy! Simply copy the flipbook of your choice (for variety and interest, you might make colored copies), distribute the pages to students, and have them follow the directions below. In three quick steps, the flipbook is completed and ready for use!

1. Carefully cut apart the flipbook pages.

2. Stack the pages.

3. Staple the pages together, then read!

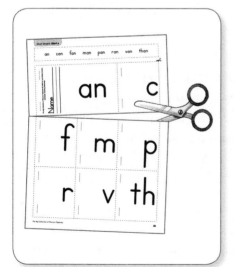

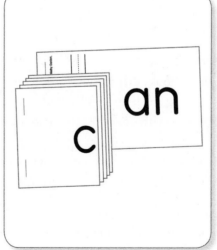

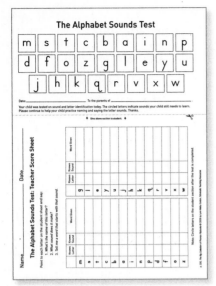

The Alphabet Sounds Test Can Help You:

- plan your phonics instruction

- decide how to group students for small group lessons

- individualize instruction

- record student learning over time

- communicate student progress with families, classroom aides, and instructional tutors

When Should I Use the Alphabet Sounds Test?

The phonics flipbooks provide terrific help for students who need practice with blending and sounding out phonetically regular words. But, if students know only the names of the letters, they are not yet ready for blending practice. In order for students to successfully sound out words, it is essential that they first master the most frequent sounds of the letters—especially the short vowel sounds. Before introducing beginning and struggling readers to any of the phonics flipbooks, use The Alphabet Sounds Test (page 220) to find out which letters and sounds they know and which still need to be taught.

To administer The Alphabet Sounds Test, copy and cut apart the two sections of the page. Fill in the student's name and date where indicated on both sections. Then give the student the top section of the test to use for his or her responses as you follow directions on the teacher section to give the test. During the test, record each response on the teacher's score sheet only. Afterward, circle the letters on the student section to indicate which ones the student needs to learn and practice. Send this section home to communicate with the student's family and encourage them to take an active role in their child's learning. You might also send a copy of the Letter-Sound Chart (page 17) for parents to use as a guide for the letter sounds.

As a reminder, if students have not yet mastered the letter sounds, plan to review or teach them in a fun, engaging, systematic, and explicit manner before using the phonics flipbooks. (See the Letter-Sound Chart on page 17.)

How Do I Use the Flipbooks With Students?

Students who have mastered letter sounds, especially the short vowel sounds, are ready to start working with phonics flipbooks to practice blending. Use the following guidelines and suggestions to help students experience success when using the flipbooks.

Start with consonant-vowel-consonant words. Present beginning readers with flipbooks that feature consonant-vowel-consonant (CVC) words containing the letters and sounds that they have already learned and mastered. Flipbooks with only the CVC pattern include those for the short vowel phonograms *-ad, -at, -et, -ig, -ip, -ob, -ox,* and *-ug.* For a complete list of flipbooks for short vowel phonograms, check the Short Vowels section under "Word Families" in the Contents (pages 3–4).

Teach blending. Preview each new word family or phonics principle. Guide students to follow along at the top of each new flipbook page as you first read the words aloud. Then help students slowly "sound out" or smoothly blend new words sound by sound. During the lesson, do the following:

The Big Collection of Phonics Flipbooks

- Encourage beginning readers to slowly and orally sound out each sound in CVC words. (Relatively slow oral blending is appropriate and most helpful for beginning readers.)

- Demonstrate a deliberate sounding-out strategy. Show students how to move their fingers from letter to letter as they blend the sounds together.

- When working with struggling students, strategically use words that start with continuous consonants such as *l, m, n, r, s, v, w,* and *z.*

- Prompt students to "keep their motor running." Model how to sustain the first sound, blend that sound into the vowel sound, and finally add the last sound. Use *"Repeat after me"* as your refrain, until students are ready to make the developmental leap and practice blending on their own.

Pick and choose flipbooks. The 200 flipbooks in this collection are designed to supplement engaging, systematic (well-sequenced), and explicit phonics lessons—not replace them. Rather than requiring students to make all the flipbooks, choose flipbooks that correspond to students' needs for additional blending practice. According to their learning styles, some students may benefit from using a greater variety of flipbooks or from using them more often for practice. The order in which you choose flipbooks for instruction might vary as well, depending on your phonics program, your teaching criteria and style, and student needs. As you use the flipbooks with students, keep in mind that effective reading instruction includes lessons related to phonemic awareness, phonics, fluency, vocabulary, and comprehension, and also integrates listening, speaking, and writing.

How Do I Use the Phonics Dictation Recording Sheet?

After introducing a new word family or phonics skill, use the Phonics Dictation Recording Sheet (page 219) to give students practice and reinforcement in sound-letter and sound-spelling relationships. Before conducting a dictation exercise, introduce the phonics generalization or featured spelling pattern that will be used in the activity. Lead students to sound out and read the words in the targeted phonics flipbook or the corresponding word strip. Then explain that they will be sounding out and writing words for practice—not taking a spelling test. (For this reason, teachers sometimes choose to leave up displays of phonogram word charts or word lists during dictation.) Assure students that it's okay to make mistakes and corrections—they will not be graded. The script at the top of page 14 provides an example of how you might conduct a dictation lesson.

> **Teaching Tip**
>
> Phonics experts strongly recommend avoiding rapid sight word drills with struggling readers, as this can encourage them to become impulsive word guessers. For students who are still learning to blend sounds together, limit sight word practice to perhaps 10–15 words (such as *the, is, are, a, to, was, for, he, she,* and *you*). The flipbooks in this collection should not be used as flashcards for rapid sight word memorization.

1. Prompt listening, speaking, and writing during the dictation exercise.

Say: *Get ready to write the sounds in the words you hear. Don't worry about making mistakes. Just listen carefully to the sounds in the words as I say them slowly and try to write what you hear. The word is _____. Everybody say _____. Good. Now write what you hear.*

2. Give immediate feedback after each word and prompt students to check their work.

Write each word on the board and say: *Now look up here at the board and check the word. If you made a mistake, fix it. If you got the word right, draw a little happy face next to it.*

3. Read all the dictated words silently and then aloud.

Say: *Now put your finger next to the first word on your list. Silently read that word to yourself. Then read the next word to yourself. Do this with all the words on your sheet. Good. Now put your finger next to the first word again. Let's read each word slowly out loud. Here we go.*

As students' blending and writing skills improve, they will also benefit from writing and reading sentences. When first introducing sentence dictation exercises, devise and use very short sentences that feature mostly three-letter CVC words, such as *pan, can, pat, cat, let, net, jog, dog, but, cut,* and so on. Try to strictly limit the use of sight words in these early sentence-writing exercises. Some good, useful beginning sight words include *the, is, are, a, to, was, for, he, she,* and *you.* Here are some examples of the type of very basic dictation sentences you might use with beginning readers and writers:

> *The dog is hot.*
> *The cat can run.*
> *The bug is sad.*

After each dictated sentence, help students check, correct, and read their writing. You can develop more complex dictation sentences based on the new phonograms and word families as they are taught.

Conducting Dictation

During a dictation exercise, do the following:

- Slowly pronounce each word one at a time. Prompt students to repeat each word and write what they hear, sound by sound on the sheet.

- Provide immediate feedback by displaying the proper spelling of each dictated word after students write it. Encourage students to check their work and correct their mistakes.

- At the end of a dictation exercise, have students read each word on their dictation sheet silently, and then aloud.

How Do I Use the Phonics Skills Tests?

The 20 Phonics Skills Tests (pages 221–240) can be used to monitor student learning and progress. They also serve as useful tools for guiding your phonics instruction and communicating with families. The handy one-page design allows you to send home one part to parents and retain the other section for your records. After students learn the skill or skills targeted on each Phonics Skill Test, follow these steps to use the test:

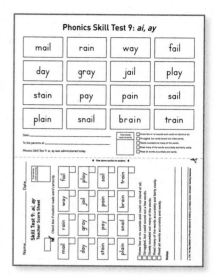

1. Copy and cut apart the two sections of the page. Fill in the student's name and date where indicated on both sections.

2. Place the top section of the test in front of the student. Ask the student to read each word one at a time. On the Teacher Score Sheet only, check the box for each word the student reads correctly.

3. After the student completes the test, count how many correct words he or she read. Write that number in the box labeled "Total words read correctly" at the top of the Teacher Score Sheet.

4. Use the key at the bottom of the score sheet to determine the level of fluency with which the student read the words. Check the box next to the most accurate description of the student's performance. Record any notes on the lines at the bottom of the sheet.

5. On the student section of the test, check each word he or she read correctly. Transfer the remaining information from the Teacher Score Sheet to the student section.

6. Send the student section home to inform families of their student's skill, progress, and needs. Keep the Teacher Score Sheet for your records.

What Are Some Ways I Can Extend Phonics Learning?

Listed below are just a few ways you can extend the use of your phonics flipbooks and provide fun, engaging activities that motivate and reinforce student learning.

Illustrate the Flipbooks. Allow students to draw pictures on the back of the pages in their flipbooks to illustrate the meaning of as many words as possible.

Make Word Bracelets. Invite students to cut out the word strip at the top of each phonics flipbook page and make bracelets with them. They can fit the strip to their wrist and then tapes the ends together. Encourage students to read and reread the words on their bracelets throughout the day. They can also wear their bracelets home to share with their families!

Create a Flipbooks Center. Place a tub of file folders containing flipbook patterns in a center. Add scissors and staplers. Then allow students to make new phonics flipbooks whenever they have spare time or as a reward.

Create Interactive Bulletin Boards. Make a 3-D interactive display by attaching phonics flipbooks to a bulletin board! Pin each flipbook to the display, leaving the pages loose to allow students to turn the pages and read the words.

Use the Flipbook Patterns in a Pocket Chart. Cut apart the pattern for the flipbooks of your choice and use the pages in a pocket chart. Invite students to move the pages around in the chart to create new and different words to sound out and spell.

Create Stories and Poems. To help build vocabulary and word usage, challenge students to use the flipbook words to tell or write their own silly or serious stories and poems. Students will enjoy working with the rhyming or alliterative flipbook words—and sharing their creations with the class!

Create Games. The words in the word family flipbooks can be used in a wide variety of easy-to-make games, such as Bingo, Go Fish, Memory, word sorts, and so on. You can even involve students in making the game cards and establishing game rules.

Make Giant Flipbooks. Make enlarged copies of the flipbook patterns and invite students to make large versions of the books. Use the giant flipbooks for whole-class lessons.

Make Nonsense Words. Allow students to play with letters and sounds from different flipbooks to invent non-words or nonsense words. Such word play can provide valuable reinforcement and practice with core phonemic awareness and phonics skills.

Connect to Literature. Be on the lookout for aspects of word play, word families, phonograms, and so on as you share read-aloud books or literature from your basal reading program. Where possible, introduce flipbooks that complement the text. This will help students make literature connections, as well as enrich your language arts program.

Link to Decodable Books. If your basal reading program features decodable or sound-out-able reading books for beginning readers, you might use the phonics flipbooks that correspond to the featured word patterns to provide additional reinforcement.

Create a Flipbooks Collection. Provide each student with a large envelope labeled "[Student's Name] Phonics Flipbook Collection." Store all the envelopes in a tub or basket in the classroom. Invite students to deposit their completed flipbooks into their envelopes for easy storage and safekeeping. Each time they make a new flipbook, send the envelope and a note home with students explaining to families how to use the flipbooks to reinforce their students' learning. For example, the note might say, "Ask your child to read the new flipbook out loud three times. Then have your child read all the other flipbooks once. Be sure to return this envelope and all flipbooks to school tomorrow. Happy Reading!"

Letter-Sound Chart

This chart features the primary (most frequent) letter sounds and words that can be used to teach them. When students are first learning letter-sound relationships, they should always be taught the primary sound for each letter.

A a   says /ă/ like we hear at the beginning of *a-a-apple*.

B b   says /b/ like we hear at the beginning of *b-b-boy*.

C c   says /k/ like we hear at the beginning of *c-c-cat*.

D d   says /d/ like we hear at the beginning of *d-d-dinosaur*.

E e   says /ĕ/ like we hear at the beginning of *e-e-elephant*.

F f   says /f/ like we hear at the beginning of *f-f-fish*.

G g   says /g/ like we hear at the beginning of *g-g-girl*.

H h   says /h/ like we hear at the beginning of *h-h-horse*.

I i   says /ĭ/ like we hear at the beginning of *i-i-insect*.

J j   says /j/ like we hear at the beginning of *j-j-jellyfish*.

K k   says /k/ like we hear at the beginning of *k-k-kangaroo*.

L l   says /l/ like we hear at the beginning of *l-l-lion*.

M m   says /m/ like we hear at the beginning of *m-m-monkey*.

N n   says /n/ like we hear at the beginning of *n-n-nose*.

O o   says /ŏ/ like we hear at the beginning of *o-o-octopus*.

P p   says /p/ like we hear at the beginning of *p-p-pig*.

Q q   says /kw/ like we hear at the beginning of *qu-qu-queen*.

R r   says /r/ like we hear at the beginning of *r-r-rabbit*.

S s   says /s/ like we hear at the beginning of *s-s-sun*.

T t   says /t/ like we hear at the beginning of *t-t-tiger*.

U u   says /ŭ/ like we hear at the beginning of *u-u-umbrella*.

V v   says /v/ like we hear at the beginning of *v-v-violin*.

W w   says /w/ like we hear at the beginning of *w-w-wagon*.

X x   says /ks/ like we hear at the end of *ax*.

Y y   says /y/ like we hear at the beginning of *y-y-yellow*.

Z z   says /z/ like we hear at the beginning of *z-z-zipper*.

References and Resources

Adams, M. (1990). *Beginning to read: Thinking and learning about print.* Cambridge, MA: MIT Press.

Bear, D. R., Invernizzi, M., Templeton, S. & Johnston, F. (2008). *Words their way: Word study for phonics, vocabulary, and spelling instruction* (4th ed.). Upper Saddle River, NJ: Pearson.

Blevins, W. (2006). *Phonics from A to Z* (2nd ed.). New York: Scholastic Professional Books.

Chall, J. & Popp, H. (1999). *Teaching and assessing phonics: Why, what, when, how.* Cambridge, MA: Educators Publishing Service.

Flesch, R. (1955, reprint 1986). *Why Johnny can't read: And what you can do about it.* New York: Perennial.

Gunning, T. G. (2000). *Phonological awareness and primary phonics.* Needham Heights, MA: Allyn & Bacon.

Hiskes, D. G. (2005). *Phonics Pathways* (9th ed.). San Francisco: Jossey-Bass.

National Institute of Child Health and Human Development. (2000). *Report of the National Reading Panel. Teaching children to read: An evidence-based assessment of the scientific research literature on reading and its implications for reading instruction.* Washington, DC: Government Printing Office.

Resnick, L. B. (Ed.) (2004). English language learners: Boosting academic achievement. *Research Points* [Special issue.] Washington, DC: American Educational Research Association, 1-4.

Shaywitz, S. (2003). *Overcoming dyslexia: A new and complete science-based program for reading problems at any level.* New York: Knopf.

Snow, C. E., Burns, M. S. & Griffin, P. (Eds.). (1998). *Preventing reading difficulties in young children.* Washington, DC: National Academy Press.

Temple, E. (2003). Changes in brain function in children with dyslexia after training. *The Phonics Bulletin: The annual newsletter of the International Reading Association's Phonics Special Interest Group*, 1, 1-3.

White, T. (2005). Effects of systematic and strategic analogy-based phonics on grade 2 students' word reading and reading comprehension. *Reading Research Quarterly*, 40, 234-255.

Wylie, R. E. & Durrell, D. D. (1970). *Elementary English*, 47, 787-791.

Helpful Websites

eric.ed.gov (Educational Resources Information Center, an online digital library of educational research and information sponsored by the U.S. Department of Education)

nrrf.org (The National Right to Read Foundation)

phonics.info (Dr. Lynn Gordon's phonics website)

phonicsbulletin.info (information and resources from the International Reading Association's Phonics Special Interest Group)

readingrockets.org (information and resources on reading sponsored by the U.S. Department of Education)

cab   jab   lab   crab   grab   scab   stab

Name

ab

c

j

l cr

gr sc st

back   Jack   pack   sack   black   crack   snack

The Big Collection of Phonics Flipbooks © 2009 by Lynn Melby Gordon, Scholastic Teaching Resources

Name

ack   b

J   p   s

bl   cr   sn

ad   bad   Dad   fad   had   mad   sad   glad

Name

ad

b

D

f

h

m

s

gl

bag   rag   sag   tag   wag   brag   flag

The Big Collection of Phonics Flipbooks © 2009 by Lynn Melby Gordon, Scholastic Teaching Resources

Name

ag

b

r

s

t

w

br

fl

am   ham   jam   Pam   Sam   yam   clam   swam

The Big Collection of Phonics Flipbooks © 2009 by Lynn Melby Gordon, Scholastic Teaching Resources

Name

am

h

j

P

S

y

cl

sw

amp camp damp lamp ramp champ clamp stamp

Name

amp

c

d

l

r

ch

cl

st

The Big Collection of Phonics Flipbooks

an   can   fan   man   pan   ran   van   than

Name

an

c

f

m

p

r

v

th

and   band   hand   land   sand   bland   brand   stand

The Big Collection of Phonics Flipbooks © 2009 by Lynn Melby Gordon, Scholastic Teaching Resources

Name

and

b

h

l

s

bl

br

st

bang   fang   gang   hang   rang   sang   slang

Name

ang

b

f

g

h

r

s

sl

bank   sank   blank   drank   Frank   spank   thank

Name

ank

b

s

bl

dr

Fr

sp

th

28

ant   pant   rant   chant   grant   plant   slant

The Big Collection of Phonics Flipbooks © 2009 by Lynn Melby Gordon, Scholastic Teaching Resources

Name

ant

p   r   ch

gr   pl   sl

cap   lap   map   nap   sap   snap   trap

Name

ap

c

l

m

n

s

sn

tr

ash cash lash mash rash flash smash trash

Name

ash

c

l

m

r

fl

sm

tr

cast   fast   last   mast   past   vast   blast

Name

ast

c

f

l   m

p   v   bl

at bat cat fat hat pat rat sat

The Big Collection of Phonics Flipbooks © 2009 by Lynn Melby Gordon, Scholastic Teaching Resources

Name

at

b

c

f

h

p

r

s

batch   catch   hatch   latch   match   patch   snatch

Name

atch   b

c   h   l

m   p   sn

34

ax   fax   lax   Max   tax   wax   flax

Name

ax

f   l   M

t   w   fl

deck   neck   peck   check   fleck   speck

Name

eck

d

n

p

ch

fl

sp

bed   fed   led   red   wed   bled   sled

Name

ed

b

f

l

r

w

bl

sl

bell   fell   sell   well   yell   smell   spell

Name

ell

b

f

s

w

y

sm

sp

belt   felt   melt   pelt   welt   dwelt

Name

elt

b   f   m

p   w   dw

den   hen   men   pen   ten   then   when

Name

en

d

h

m

p

t

th

wh

bench   drench   French   quench   stench   trench

Name

ench

b

dr

Fr

qu

st

tr

end   bend   lend   mend   send   blend   spend   trend

The Big Collection of Phonics Flipbooks © 2009 by Lynn Melby Gordon, Scholastic Teaching Resources

Name

end

b

l   m   s

bl   sp   tr

bent   dent   rent   sent   tent   went   spent

Name

ent   b

d   r   s

t   w   sp

kept   wept   crept   slept   swept

Name

ept

k   w   cr

sl   sw

44

less   mess   chess   dress   guess   press   stress

Name

ess   l

m   ch   dr

gu   pr   str

best   nest   pest   rest   test   vest   west

Name

est   b

n   p   r

t   v   w

get   jet   let   met   net   pet   wet

Name

e t

g

j

l

m

n

p

w

bib   fib   jib   nib   rib   crib   glib

Name

ib

b

f

j

n

r

cr

gl

48

kick   lick   pick   sick   quick   stick   trick

Name

ick

k

l

p

s

qu

st

tr

did   hid   kid   lid   rid   grid   slid

Name

id

d

h

k

l

r

gr

sl

gift   lift   sift   drift   shift   swift   thrift

The Big Collection of Phonics Flipbooks © 2009 by Lynn Melby Gordon, Scholastic Teaching Resources

Name

ift

g

l

s

dr

sh

sw

thr

big   dig   fig   gig   jig   pig   wig

Name

ig

b

d

f

g

j

p

w

ill   bill   fill   gill   hill   Jill   will   still

Name

ill

b

f

g

h

J

w

st

dim   him   Jim   Kim   slim   swim   trim

The Big Collection of Phonics Flipbooks © 2009 by Lynn Melby Gordon, Scholastic Teaching Resources

Name

im

d

h

J

K

sl

sw

tr

54

imp   limp   chimp   crimp   primp   skimp   shrimp

Name

imp

l   ch   cr

pr   sk   shr

in   fin   pin   win   chin   skin   thin   twin

Name

in

f

p

w

ch

sk

th

tw

king   ring   sing   wing   bring   sting   thing

Name

ing   k

r   s   w

br   st   th

ink pink sink wink blink drink stink think

Name

ink

p

s

w

bl

dr

st

th

hint   lint   mint   tint   print   splint   squint

Name

int

h

l

m

t

pr   spl   squ

dip   hip   lip   rip   sip   tip   zip

Name

ip

d

h

l

r

s

t

z

60

it   bit   fit   hit   pit   sit   quit   spit

The Big Collection of Phonics Flipbooks © 2009 by Lynn Melby Gordon, Scholastic Teaching Resources

Name _____

it

b

f

h

p

s

qu

sp

itch   ditch   hitch   pitch   witch   glitch   stitch   switch

Name

itch

d

h

p

w

gl

st

sw

Bob   cob   gob   job   mob   rob   sob

Name

ob   B

c   g   j

m   r   s

dock   lock   rock   sock   block   clock   flock

The Big Collection of Phonics Flipbooks © 2009 by Lynn Melby Gordon, Scholastic Teaching Resources

Name

ock

d

l

r

s

bl

cl

fl

cod   mod   nod   pod   rod   clod   plod

The Big Collection of Phonics Flipbooks © 2009 by Lynn Melby Gordon, Scholastic Teaching Resources

Name

od

c

m

n

p

r

cl

pl

dog   fog   hog   jog   log   clog   frog

The Big Collection of Phonics Flipbooks © 2009 by Lynn Melby Gordon, Scholastic Teaching Resources

Name

og

d

f

h

j

l

cl

fr

cop   hop   mop   pop   top   drop   stop

Name

op

c

h

m

p

t

dr

st

dot   got   hot   lot   not   pot   spot

Name

ot

d

g

h

l

n

p

sp

68

ox   box   fox   lox   pox

Name

ox

b

f

l

p

cub   hub   rub   sub   tub   club   scrub

Name

ub

c

h

r

s

t

cl

scr

70

bud   cud   dud   mud   crud   spud   thud

Name

ud   b

c   d   m

cr   sp   th

duck   luck   puck   suck   tuck   stuck   truck

The Big Collection of Phonics Flipbooks © 2009 by Lynn Melby Gordon, Scholastic Teaching Resources

Name

uck   d

l   p   s

t   st   tr

buff   cuff   huff   puff   fluff   scuff   stuff

Name

uff

b

c

h

p

fl

sc

st

bug   dug   hug   jug   mug   rug   tug

Name

ug

b

d

h

j

m

r

t

gum   hum   rum   sum   chum   drum   plum

Name

um

g

h

r

s

ch

dr

pl

bump   dump   hump   jump   lump   pump   thump

Name

ump

b

d

h

j

l

p

th

bun   fun   gun   pun   run   sun   spun

The Big Collection of Phonics Flipbooks © 2009 by Lynn Melby Gordon, Scholastic Teaching Resources

Name

un

b

f

g

p

r

s

sp

bunch lunch munch punch brunch crunch scrunch

The Big Collection of Phonics Flipbooks © 2009 by Lynn Melby Gordon, Scholastic Teaching Resources

Name

unch

b

l

m

p

br

cr

scr

hung lung sung clung slung sprung strung

Name

ung

h

l

s

cl

sl

spr

str

bunk   hunk   junk   sunk   drunk   skunk   trunk

Name

unk

b

h

j

s

dr

sk

tr

bunt   hunt   punt   runt   blunt   grunt   stunt

Name

unt

b

h

p

r

bl

gr

st

hush   mush   rush   blush   brush   crush   flush

Name

ush

h

m

r

bl

br

cr

fl

The Big Collection of Phonics Flipbooks

dust   gust   just   must   rust   crust   trust

Name

ust   d

g   j   m

r   cr   tr

but   cut   gut   hut   nut   rut   shut

Name

ut

b

c

g

h

n

r

sh

84

ace   face   lace   race   brace   place   space   trace

Name

ace

f

l

r

br

pl

sp

tr

fade   made   wade   blade   grade   shade   trade

Name

ade

f

m

w

bl

gr

sh

tr

age   cage   page   rage   sage   wage   stage

Name

age

c   p   r

s   w   st

bake   cake   lake   make   take   wake   snake

The Big Collection of Phonics Flipbooks © 2009 by Lynn Melby Gordon, Scholastic Teaching Resources

Name

ake

b

c

l

m

t

w

sn

ale   male   pale   sale   tale   scale   stale   whale

The Big Collection of Phonics Flipbooks © 2009 by Lynn Melby Gordon, Scholastic Teaching Resources

Name

ale   m

p   s   t

sc   st   wh

came game name same blame flame frame

Name

ame   c

g   n   s

bl   fl   fr

cane   Jane   lane   mane   pane   crane   plane

Name _____

ane

c

J

l

m

p

cr

pl

ape   cape   gape   tape   drape   grape   scrape   shape

The Big Collection of Phonics Flipbooks © 2009 by Lynn Melby Gordon, Scholastic Teaching Resources

Name

ape   c

g   t   dr

gr   scr   sh

92

ate   date   gate   hate   late   plate   skate   state

Name

ate

d

g

h

l

pl

sk

st

cave   Dave   gave   save   wave   brave   grave

Name

ave   c

D   g   s

w   br   gr

daze   gaze   haze   maze   blaze   craze   glaze

The Big Collection of Phonics Flipbooks © 2009 by Lynn Melby Gordon, Scholastic Teaching Resources

Name

aze   d

g   h   m

bl   cr   gl

ice   dice   mice   nice   rice   price   slice   twice

The Big Collection of Phonics Flipbooks © 2009 by Lynn Melby Gordon, Scholastic Teaching Resources

Name

ice

d

m

n

r

pr

sl

tw

hide   ride   side   wide   bride   glide   slide

The Big Collection of Phonics Flipbooks © 2009 by Lynn Melby Gordon, Scholastic Teaching Resources

Name

ide

h

r

s

w

br

gl

sl

fife   life   rife   wife   strife

Name

ife

f   l   r

w str

bike   hike   like   Mike   spike   strike   trike

Name

ike

b

h

l M

sp str tr

file   mile   pile   tile   vile   smile   while

Name

ile

f

m

p

t

v

sm

wh

dime   lime   time   chime   crime   grime   slime

Name

ime

d

l

t

ch

cr

gr

sl

dine   fine   line   mine   nine   pine   vine

Name

ine

d

f

l

m

n

p

v

pipe   ripe   wipe   gripe   snipe   swipe   stripe

The Big Collection of Phonics Flipbooks © 2009 by Lynn Melby Gordon, Scholastic Teaching Resources

Name

ipe   p

r   w   gr

sn   sw   str

bite   kite   mite   site   quite   spite   white

The Big Collection of Phonics Flipbooks © 2009 by Lynn Melby Gordon, Scholastic Teaching Resources

Name

ite

b

k

m

s

qu

sp

wh

104

dive   five   hive   jive   live   drive   strive

The Big Collection of Phonics Flipbooks © 2009 by Lynn Melby Gordon, Scholastic Teaching Resources

Name

ive   d

f   h   j

l   dr   str

joke poke woke broke choke smoke spoke

The Big Collection of Phonics Flipbooks © 2009 by Lynn Melby Gordon, Scholastic Teaching Resources

Name

oke

j

p

w

br

ch

sm

sp

dole   hole   mole   pole   role   sole   stole

Name

ole   d

h   m   p

r   s   st

bone   cone   zone   clone   phone   shone   stone

The Big Collection of Phonics Flipbooks © 2009 by Lynn Melby Gordon, Scholastic Teaching Resources

Name

one

b

c

z

cl

ph

sh

st

cope   dope   hope   mope   nope   grope   scope

The Big Collection of Phonics Flipbooks © 2009 by Lynn Melby Gordon, Scholastic Teaching Resources

Name

ope   c

d   h   m

n   gr   sc

hose   nose   pose   rose   chose   close   those

Name

ose   h

n   p   r

ch   cl   th

dote   note   rote   tote   vote   quote

Name

ote

d   n   r

t   v   qu

cove   wove   clove   drove   grove   stove   trove

The Big Collection of Phonics Flipbooks © 2009 by Lynn Melby Gordon, Scholastic Teaching Resources

Name

ove

c

w

cl

dr

gr

st

tr

dude   nude   rude   crude   prude

Name

ude

d   n   r

cr   pr

cute   jute   lute   mute   brute   flute

Name

ute

c

j

l

m

br

fl

ail   fail   jail   mail   nail   pail   sail   snail

Name

ail

f

j

m

n

p

s

sn

main   pain   rain   brain   plain   stain   train

Name

ain   m

p   r   br

pl   st   tr

day   may   pay   say   way   gray   play

Name

ay

d

m

p

s

w

gr

pl

be   he   me   we   she

Name

e

b   h   m

w   sh

The Big Collection of Phonics Flipbooks

pea   sea   tea   flea   plea

Name

ea

p   s   t

fl   pl

each beach leach peach reach teach bleach preach

Name

each

b

l

p

r

t

bl

pr

120

beak   leak   peak   weak   sneak   speak   squeak

Name

eak

b

l

p

w

sn

sp

squ

deal   heal   meal   real   seal   steal   squeal

The Big Collection of Phonics Flipbooks © 2009 by Lynn Melby Gordon, Scholastic Teaching Resources

Name

eal

d

h

m

r

s

st

squ

beam team cream dream steam scream stream

The Big Collection of Phonics Flipbooks © 2009 by Lynn Melby Gordon, Scholastic Teaching Resources

Name

eam

b

t

cr

dr

st

scr

str

eat   beat   heat   meat   neat   seat   bleat   cheat

Name

eat   b

h   m   n

s   bl   ch

bee   fee   see   flee   free   tree   three

Name

ee

b

f

s

fl

fr

tr

thr

feed   need   seed   weed   bleed   greed   speed

Name

eed   f

n   s   w

bl   gr   sp

peek   seek   week   cheek   creek   Greek   sleek

Name

eek

p

s

w

ch

cr

Gr

sl

eel   feel   heel   keel   peel   reel   steel   wheel

Name

eel

f

h

k

p

r

st

wh

beep   deep   jeep   keep   weep   cheep   sleep

Name

eep

b

d

j

k

w

ch

sl

beet   feet   meet   greet   sheet   sweet   street

Name

eet

b

f

m

gr

sh

sw

str

130

fight   light   might   right   sight   tight   bright

Name

ight

f

l

m

r

s

t

br

bind   find   kind   mind   wind   blind   grind

Name

ind

b

f

k

m

w

bl

gr

oat   boat   coat   goat   moat   float   gloat   throat

The Big Collection of Phonics Flipbooks © 2009 by Lynn Melby Gordon, Scholastic Teaching Resources

Name

oat

b

c

g

m

fl

gl

thr

old   cold   fold   gold   hold   mold   sold   told

Name

old   c

f   g   h

m   s   t

134

low   mow   crow   grow   show   snow

Name

ow

l   m   cr

gr   sh   sn

own   mown   blown   flown   grown   shown   thrown

✂

Name

own

m   bl   fl

gr   sh   thr

by　my　cry　fly　sky　try　shy　why

The Big Collection of Phonics Flipbooks © 2009 by Lynn Melby Gordon, Scholastic Teaching Resources

Name

y

b　m　cr　fl

sk　tr　sh　wh

oil   boil   coil   foil   soil   toil   broil   spoil

Name

oil

b

c

f

s

t

br

sp

ouch   couch   pouch   vouch   crouch   grouch   slouch

The Big Collection of Phonics Flipbooks © 2009 by Lynn Melby Gordon, Scholastic Teaching Resources

Name

ouch

c

p

v

cr

gr

sl

bound found hound pound round sound ground

Name

ound

b

f

h

p

r

s

gr

house   louse   mouse   blouse   grouse   spouse

The Big Collection of Phonics Flipbooks © 2009 by Lynn Melby Gordon, Scholastic Teaching Resources

Name

ouse

h

l

m

bl

gr

sp

out   pout   scout   shout   spout   trout   sprout

Name

out

p   sc   sh

sp   tr   spr

The Big Collection of Phonics Flipbooks

ow   cow   how   now   vow   wow   brow   plow

The Big Collection of Phonics Flipbooks © 2009 by Lynn Melby Gordon, Scholastic Teaching Resources

Name

ow

c

h

n

v

w

br

pl

owl   fowl   howl   jowl   growl   prowl   scowl

Name

owl

f

h

j

gr

pr

sc

down town brown clown crown drown frown

Name

own

d

t

br

cl

cr

dr

fr

boy   coy   joy   Roy   soy   toy   ploy

Name

oy

b

c

j

R

s

t

pl

146

all   call   fall   mall   tall   wall   small   stall

The Big Collection of Phonics Flipbooks © 2009 by Lynn Melby Gordon, Scholastic Teaching Resources

Name

all

c

f

m

t

w

sm

st

aw   jaw   law   paw   raw   saw   draw   straw

Name

aw

j

l

p

r

s

dr

str

dawn fawn lawn pawn yawn drawn prawn

Name

awn

d

f

l

p

y

dr

pr

dew   new   blew   chew   crew   threw

Name

ew

d   n   bl

ch   cr   thr

gong   long   song   tong   prong   strong

Name

ong

g   l   s

t   pr   str

boo   coo   goo   moo   too   zoo

Name

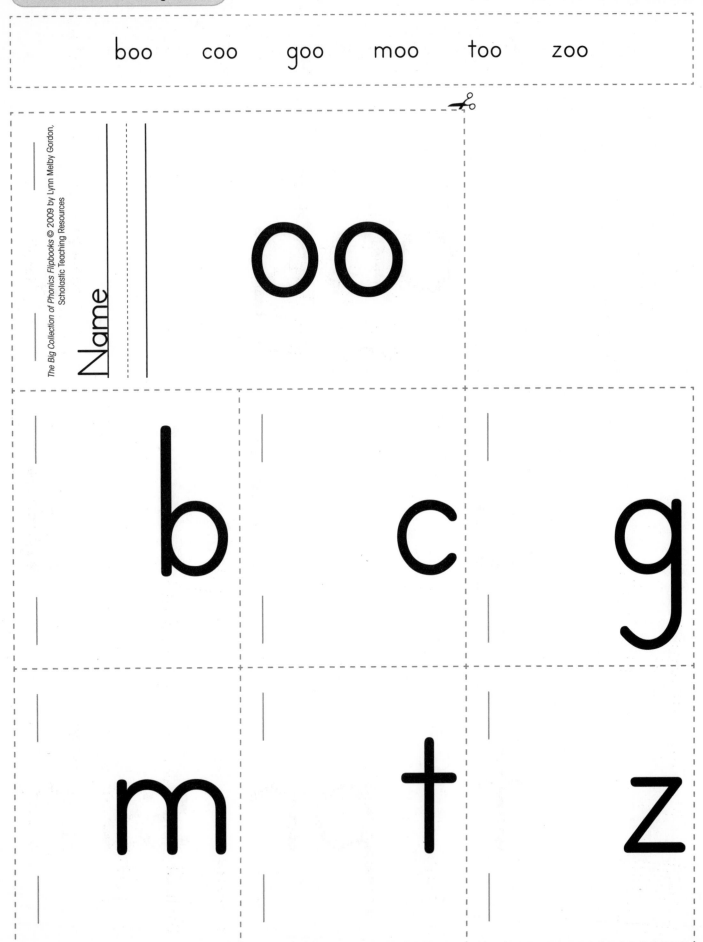

oo

b   c   g

m   t   z

book   cook   hook   look   took   brook   shook

Name

ook   b

c   h   l

t   br   sh

cool   fool   pool   tool   drool   school   stool

The Big Collection of Phonics Flipbooks © 2009 by Lynn Melby Gordon, Scholastic Teaching Resources

Name

ool

c

f

p

t

dr   sch   st

boom   room   zoom   bloom   broom   gloom   groom

Name

oom

b

r

z

bl

br

gl

gr

coop   hoop   loop   droop   scoop   snoop   troop

Name

oop   c

h   l   dr

sc   sn   tr

boot   hoot   loot   root   toot   scoot   shoot

Name

oot   b

h   l   r

t   sc   sh

boss   loss   moss   toss   cross   floss   gloss

Name

oss

b

l

m

t

cr

fl

gl

air   fair   hair   pair   chair   flair   stair

Name

air

f

h

p

ch

fl

st

bar   car   far   jar   tar   scar   star

Name

ar

b

c

f

j

t

sc

st

bare   care   rare   scare   share   stare   square

The Big Collection of Phonics Flipbooks © 2009 by Lynn Melby Gordon, Scholastic Teaching Resources

Name

are   b

c   r   sc

sh   st   squ

bark   dark   mark   park   Clark   shark   spark

Name

ark   b

d   m   p

Cl   sh   sp

162

cart   dart   part   tart   chart   smart   start

Name

art

c

d

p

t

ch

sm

st

ear   dear   fear   gear   hear   year   clear   smear

Name

ear

d

f

g

h

y

cl

sm

dirt   flirt   shirt   skirt   squirt

Name

irt

d

fl

sh

sk squ

ore   more   sore   wore   chore   score   snore   store

Name

ore   m

s   w   ch

sc   sn   st

cork   fork   pork   York   stork

Name

ork

c

f

p

Y

st

born   corn   horn   torn   worn   scorn   thorn

The Big Collection of Phonics Flipbooks © 2009 by Lynn Melby Gordon, Scholastic Teaching Resources

Name

orn   b

c   h   t

w   sc   th

fort   Mort   port   sort   short   snort   sport

Name

ort   f

M   p   s

sh   sn   sp

bled   blob   black   blast   blend   blond   blush

bl

Name

ed

ob

ack

ast

end

ond

ush

brad   bran   brat   brim   brand   brass   brick

br

Name

ad

an   at   im

and   ass   ick

clam   clap   clip   club   class   cliff   clock

cl

am

ap

ip

ub

ass

iff

ock

crab   crib   crop   crack   craft   cross   crust

cr

ab

ib

op

ack

aft

oss

ust

Name

The Big Collection of Phonics Flipbooks © 2009 by Lynn Melby Gordon, Scholastic Teaching Resources

drag   drip   drop   drug   drum   dress   drill

dr

ag

ip   op   ug

um   ess   ill

flag   flat   flip   flop   flock   floss   fluff

fl

Name

ag

at

ip

op

ock   oss   uff

fret   frog   fresh   frill   frizz   frost   free

fr

et

og   esh   ill

izz   ost   ee

glad   glop   glum   gland   glass   glint   gloss

gl

Name

The Big Collection of Phonics Flipbooks © 2009 by Lynn Melby Gordon,
Scholastic Teaching Resources

ad

op   um   and

ass   int   oss

grab   grin   grip   grit   grub   grant   grass

gr

Name

The Big Collection of Phonics Flipbooks © 2009 by Lynn Melby Gordon,
Scholastic Teaching Resources

ab

in   ip   it

ub ant ass

plan   plop   plot   plug   plum   plus   plant

pl

Name

an

op   ot   ug

um   us   ant

prim   prod   prop   press   prick   primp   print

pr

im

od   op   ess

ick   imp   int

quit   quiz   quack   quest   quick   quill   quilt

qu

it

iz

ack   est

ick   ill   ilt

scab   scan   scam   scat   scum   scoff   scuff

sc

Name

The Big Collection of Phonics Flipbooks © 2009 by Lynn Melby Gordon,
Scholastic Teaching Resources

ab

an   am   at

um   off   uff

scrap   scrub   scratch   scrape   scream   screen

The Big Collection of Phonics Flipbooks © 2009 by
Lynn Melby Gordon, Scholastic Teaching Resources

Name

scr

ap

ub

atch

ape

eam

een

skid   skin   skip   skit   skill   skull   skunk

sk

Name

The Big Collection of Phonics Flipbooks © 2009 by Lynn Melby Gordon, Scholastic Teaching Resources

id

in

ip

it

ill

ull

unk

slam   slap   slid   slip   slug   slant   slept

sl

Name

The Big Collection of Phonics Flipbooks © 2009 by Lynn Melby Gordon,
Scholastic Teaching Resources

am

ap   id   ip

ug   ant   ept

smug   smack   smash   smell   smelt   smock

sm

Name

The Big Collection of Phonics Flipbooks © 2009
by Lynn Melby Gordon, Scholastic Teaching Resources

ug

ack

ash

ell

elt

ock

snap   snip   snob   snub   snug   snack   sniff

sn

Name

The Big Collection of Phonics Flipbooks © 2009 by Lynn Melby Gordon, Scholastic Teaching Resources

ap

ip

ob

ub

ug

ack

iff

squid   squint   squish   squeak   squeal   squeeze   square

squ

Name

The Big Collection of Phonics Flipbooks © 2009 by Lynn Melby Gordon,
Scholastic Teaching Resources

id

int   ish   eak

eal   eeze   are

spin   spit   spot   spell   spend   spent   spill

sp

Name

in

it

ot

ell

end ent ill

splat   split   splash   splint   splosh   splotch

The Big Collection of Phonics Flipbooks © 2009
by Lynn Melby Gordon, Scholastic Teaching Resources

Name

spl

at

it

ash

int

osh

otch

step   stop   stamp   stand   stick   stiff   still

Name

st

ep

op

amp

and

ick

iff

ill

strap   strip   stress   string   strong   struck   street

str

Name

ap

ip

ess

ing

ong

uck

eet

swam   swim   swell   swept   swing   swish   switch

sw

Name

The Big Collection of Phonics Flipbooks © 2009 by Lynn Melby Gordon,
Scholastic Teaching Resources

am

im   ell   ept

ing   ish   itch

trap   trim   trip   trot   track   truck   trust

tr

Name

The Big Collection of Phonics Flipbooks © 2009 by Lynn Melby Gordon,
Scholastic Teaching Resources

ap

im

ip

ot

ack

uck

ust

194

twig   twin   twitch   twice   twine   tweed   tweet

tw

Name

The Big Collection of Phonics Flipbooks © 2009 by Lynn Melby Gordon,
Scholastic Teaching Resources

ig

in   itch ice

ine   eed eet

chat   chin   chop   check   chest   chick   chill

ch

Name

The Big Collection of Phonics Flipbooks © 2009 by Lynn Melby Gordon,
Scholastic Teaching Resources

at

in   op   eck

est   ick   ill

shin   ship   shop   shut   shack   shell   shock

sh

Name

The Big Collection of Phonics Flipbooks © 2009 by Lynn Melby Gordon, Scholastic Teaching Resources

in

ip

op

ut

ack

ell

ock

than   that   them   then   this   these   those

th

Name

The Big Collection of Phonics Flipbooks © 2009 by Lynn Melby Gordon,
Scholastic Teaching Resources

an

at   em   en

is   ese   ose

thin   thud   thank   thick   think   thing   thump

th

Name

The Big Collection of Phonics Flipbooks © 2009 by Lynn Melby Gordon,
Scholastic Teaching Resources

in

ud   ank   ick

ink   ing   ump

throb thrash thrill thrush three throat throw

thr

Name

The Big Collection of Phonics Flipbooks © 2009 by Lynn Melby Gordon, Scholastic Teaching Resources

ob

ash ill ush

ee oat ow

why   when   whip   which   whale   white   wheel

wh

Name

The Big Collection of Phonics Flipbooks © 2009 by Lynn Melby Gordon, Scholastic Teaching Resources

y

en   ip   ich

ale   ite   eel

disobey   dislike   disagree   discover   disinfect   displace

dis

Name

The Big Collection of Phonics Flipbooks © 2009
by Lynn Melby Gordon, Scholastic Teaching Resources

obey   like

agree   cover

infect   place

prepay precook pretest preview premature preschool

pre

pay

cook

test

view

mature school

redo   react   refill   remove   return   replay

re

Name

The Big Collection of Phonics Flipbooks © 2009
by Lynn Melby Gordon, Scholastic Teaching Resources

do

act

fill

move

turn

play

submarine subdivide subtest suburban subway

sub

Name

The Big Collection of Phonics Flipbooks © 2009
by Lynn Melby Gordon, Scholastic Teaching Resources

marine divide

test urban

way

unzip unkind unlock uncover unhappy unlucky

Name

The Big Collection of Phonics Flipbooks
by Lynn Melby Gordon, Scholastic Teaching Resources © 2009

un

zip

kind

lock

cover

happy

lucky

called fizzed pulled yelled mailed spilled stormed

Name

ed

call

fizz

pull

yell

mail

spill

storm

mixed   cooked   kicked   kissed   helped   fished   wished

The Big Collection of Phonics Flipbooks © 2009 by Lynn Melby Gordon, Scholastic Teaching Resources

Name

ed

mix

cook   kick   kiss

help   fish   wish

dented landed listed melted needed tested planted

Name

ed

dent

land

list

melt

need

test

plant

golfer   helper   painter   pitcher   singer   teacher

The Big Collection of Phonics Flipbooks © 2009
by Lynn Melby Gordon, Scholastic Teaching Resources

Name

er

golf   help

paint   pitch

sing   teach

210

careful helpful hopeful painful playful respectful

*The Big Collection of Phonics Flipbooks © 2009
by Lynn Melby Gordon, Scholastic Teaching Resources*

Name

ful

care

help

hope

pain

play

respect

doing acting saying calling looking telling spelling

Name

ing

do

act

say

call

look

tell

spell

The Big Collection of Phonics Flipbooks

jobless   fearless   helpless   homeless   hopeless   sleepless

*The Big Collection of Phonics Flipbooks © 2009
by Lynn Melby Gordon, Scholastic Teaching Resources*

Name

less

job

fear

help

home

hope

sleep

gladly   neatly   rudely   safely   softly   quietly

The Big Collection of Phonics Flipbooks © 2009
by Lynn Melby Gordon, Scholastic Teaching Resources

Name

ly

glad

neat

rude

safe

soft

quiet

shipment payment treatment agreement excitement punishment

Name

ment

ship

pay

treat

agree

excite

punish

cats   cuts   hops   lips   naps   pets   zips

Name

s

cat

cut   hop

lip

nap   pet

zip

bags   beds   bugs   cans   kids   hogs   hugs

Name

s

bag

bed   bug   can

kid   hog   hug

dirty   dusty   sandy   brainy   glassy   frosty   sleepy

Name _____

y

dirt

dust   sand   brain

glass   frost   sleep

Name

Date

Phonics Dictation

1

2

3

4

5

6

7

8

Name

Date

Phonics Dictation

1

2

3

4

5

6

7

8

The Alphabet Sounds Test

m	s	t	c	b	a	i	n	p

d	f	o	z	g	l	e	y	u

j	h	k	q	r	v	x	w

Date:_____ To the parents of _____ .

Your child was tested on sound and letter identification today. The circled letters indicate sounds your child still needs to learn. Please continue to help your child practice naming and saying the letter sounds. Thanks.

- -

↑ **Give above section to student.** ↑

Name_____   Date_____

The Alphabet Sounds Test: Teacher Score Sheet

Point to each letter on the student sheet and say:

1. *What's the name of this letter?*
2. *What sound does it make?*
3. *Tell me a word that starts with that sound.*

	Knows Letter	Knows Sound	Word Given
m			
s			
t			
c			
b			
a			
i			
n			
p			
d			
f			
o			
z			

	Knows Letter	Knows Sound	Word Given
g			
l			
e			
y			
u			
j			
h			
k			
q			
r			
v			
x			
w			

Note: Circle letters on the student section after the test is completed.

Phonics Skill Test 1: Short *a*

cab	sad	jam	Sam
cat	lap	wax	ant
and	van	clam	swam
fast	lamp	flag	black

Date:_____

To the parents of _____ .

Phonics Skill Test 1: Short a *was administered today.*

Total words read correctly

☐ Knew few or no sounds and could not blend at all.
☐ Struggled, but could sound out a few words.
☐ Slowly sounded out many of the words.
☐ Read many of the words accurately and fairly easily.
☐ Read all words accurately and easily.

- ✂ - - -

⬆ **Give above section to student.** ⬆

Name_____

Date_____

Total words read correctly

Skill Test 1: Short *a*
Teacher Score Sheet

✓ Check box if student reads word correctly

cab	sad	jam	Sam
cat	lap	wax	ant
and	van	clam	swam
fast	lamp	flag	black

☐ Knew few or no sounds and could not blend at all.
☐ Struggled, but could sound out a few words.
☐ Slowly sounded out many of the words.
☐ Read many of the words accurately and fairly easily.
☐ Read all words accurately and easily.

Notes

Phonics Skill Test 2: Short *e*

bed	hen	jet	red
pet	spell	bend	deck
wept	mess	rest	felt
neck	yell	when	sent

Date:_____

To the parents of _____ .

Phonics Skill Test 2: Short e was administered today.

Total words
read correctly

- [ ] Knew few or no sounds and could not blend at all.
- [ ] Struggled, but could sound out a few words.
- [ ] Slowly sounded out many of the words.
- [ ] Read many of the words accurately and fairly easily.
- [ ] Read all words accurately and easily.

⬆ **Give above section to student.** ⬆

Name _____

Date _____

Skill Test 2: Short *e*
Teacher Score Sheet

✓ *Check box if student reads word correctly.*

Total words
read correctly

bed	hen	jet	red
pet	spell	bend	deck
wept	mess	rest	felt
neck	yell	when	sent

- [ ] Knew few or no sounds and could not blend at all.
- [ ] Struggled, but could sound out a few words.
- [ ] Slowly sounded out many of the words.
- [ ] Read many of the words accurately and fairly easily.
- [ ] Read all words accurately and easily.

Notes

Phonics Skill Test 3: Short *i*

rib	kid	pig	ill
him	fin	tip	sit
zip	will	swim	gift
mint	twin	trick	quit

Date:_____

To the parents of _____ .

Phonics Skill Test 3: Short i *was administered today.*

Total words
read correctly

☐ Knew few or no sounds and could not blend at all.
☐ Struggled, but could sound out a few words.
☐ Slowly sounded out many of the words.
☐ Read many of the words accurately and fairly easily.
☐ Read all words accurately and easily.

▲ **Give above section to student.** ▲ ✄

Name_____   Date_____

Skill Test 3: Short *i*
Teacher Score Sheet

Total words
read correctly

✓ *Check box if student reads word correctly.*

☐

rib	kid	pig	ill
him	fin	tip	sit
zip	will	swim	gift
mint	twin	trick	quit

☐ Knew few or no sounds and could not blend at all.
☐ Struggled, but could sound out a few words.
☐ Slowly sounded out many of the words.
☐ Read many of the words accurately and fairly easily.
☐ Read all words accurately and easily.

Notes

p. 223, *The Big Collection of Phonics Flipbooks* © 2009 by Lynn Melby Gordon, Scholastic Teaching Resources

Phonics Skill Test 4: Short *o*

job	ox	fog	hop
got	pox	rob	nod
cob	log	drop	frog
flock	spot	plod	clock

Date:_____

To the parents of _____ .

Phonics Skill Test 4: Short o *was administered today.*

Total words read correctly

- [ ] Knew few or no sounds and could not blend at all.
- [ ] Struggled, but could sound out a few words.
- [ ] Slowly sounded out many of the words.
- [ ] Read many of the words accurately and fairly easily.
- [ ] Read all words accurately and easily.

⬆ **Give above section to student.** ⬆ ✂

Name _____

Date _____

Skill Test 4: Short *o*
Teacher Score Sheet

Check box if student reads word correctly.

job	ox	hop	
got	pox	fog	
cob	log	rob	
flock	spot	drop	
		frog	
		plod	
		clock	

Total words read correctly

- [ ] Knew few or no sounds and could not blend at all.
- [ ] Struggled, but could sound out a few words.
- [ ] Slowly sounded out many of the words.
- [ ] Read many of the words accurately and fairly easily.
- [ ] Read all words accurately and easily.

Notes

Phonics Skill Test 5: Short *u*

tub	mud	hug	gum
fun	cut	run	hunt
club	duck	jump	luck
just	stuff	truck	scrub

Date:_____

To the parents of _____ .

Phonics Skill Test 5: Short u *was administered today.*

Total words read correctly

- ☐ Knew few or no sounds and could not blend at all.
- ☐ Struggled, but could sound out a few words.
- ☐ Slowly sounded out many of the words.
- ☐ Read many of the words accurately and fairly easily.
- ☐ Read all words accurately and easily.

Name_____

Date_____

Skill Test 5: Short *u*
Teacher Score Sheet

Total words read correctly

✓ *Check box if student reads word correctly.*

tub	mud	hug	gum
fun	cut	run	hunt
club	duck	jump	luck
just	stuff	truck	scrub

- ☐ Knew few or no sounds and could not blend at all.
- ☐ Struggled, but could sound out a few words.
- ☐ Slowly sounded out many of the words.
- ☐ Read many of the words accurately and fairly easily.
- ☐ Read all words accurately and easily.

Notes

Phonics Skill Test 6: Silly Words

sab	pef	jid	rox
cug	yan	kez	hib
lom	wum	ques	tiv

Date:_____

To the parents of _____

Phonics Skill Test 6: Silly Words was administered today.

Total words read correctly

☐ Knew few or no sounds and could not blend at all.

☐ Struggled, but could sound out a few words.

☐ Slowly sounded out many of the words.

☐ Read many of the words accurately and fairly easily.

☐ Read all words accurately and easily.

▲ **Give above section to student.** ▲

Name _____ Date _____

Total words read correctly

Skill Test 6: Silly Words
Teacher Score Sheet

Say: *This game is called Silly Words because none of these words are real words. Let's see how many of these words you can read. Think about the sounds of the letters and just try to sound out the words as best you can.*

Circle the small box for each letter sound the student misses or mispronounces.

sab			pef			jid			rox		
s	a	b	p	e	f	j	i	d	r	o	x

cug			yan			kez			hib		
c	u	g	y	a	n	k	e	z	h	i	b

lom			wum			ques			tiv		
l	o	m	w	u	m	qu	e	s	t	i	v

Summary: *Circle all the missed letters from above.*

a b c d e f g h i j k l m
n o p q r s t u v w x y z

☐ Knew few or no sounds and could not blend at all.
☐ Struggled, but could sound out a few words.
☐ Slowly sounded out many of the words.
☐ Read many of the words accurately and fairly easily.
☐ Read all words accurately and easily.

Phonics Skill Test 7: Silent *e* (Long *a* and *i*)

make	same	tape	gave
face	blade	page	lane
ripe	hide	bike	smile
wife	nice	dime	jive

Date:_____

To the parents of _____ .

Phonics Skill Test 7: Silent e *(Long* a *and* i*) was administered today.*

Total words read correctly

☐ Knew few or no sounds and could not blend at all.
☐ Struggled, but could sound out a few words.
☐ Slowly sounded out many of the words.
☐ Read many of the words accurately and fairly easily.
☐ Read all words accurately and easily.

⬆ **Give above section to student.** ⬆ ✂

Name _____

Date _____

Skill Test 7: Silent *e* (Long *a* and *i*)
Teacher Score Sheet

✔ *Check box if student reads word correctly.*

Total words read correctly

make	same	tape	gave
face	blade	page	lane
ripe	hide	bike	smile
wife	nice	dime	jive

☐ Knew few or no sounds and could not blend at all.
☐ Struggled, but could sound out a few words.
☐ Slowly sounded out many of the words.
☐ Read many of the words accurately and fairly easily.
☐ Read all words accurately and easily.

Notes

Phonics Skill Test 8: Silent *e* (Long *o* and *u*)

pole	bone	woke	rose
note	joke	zone	stove
hope	vote	scope	dude
lute	rude	cute	flute

Date:_____

To the parents of _____ .

Phonics Skill Test 8: Silent e *(Long* o *and* u*) was administered today.*

Total words read correctly

☐ Knew few or no sounds and could not blend at all.
☐ Struggled, but could sound out a few words.
☐ Slowly sounded out many of the words.
☐ Read many of the words accurately and fairly easily.
☐ Read all words accurately and easily.

▲ Give above section to student. ▲

Name_____

Date_____

Skill Test 8: Silent *e* (Long *o* and *u*)
Teacher Score Sheet

☑ *Check box if student reads word correctly.*

pole ☐	bone ☐	woke ☐	rose ☐
note ☐	joke ☐	zone ☐	stove ☐
hope ☐	vote ☐	scope ☐	dude ☐
lute ☐	rude ☐	cute ☐	flute ☐

Total words read correctly

☐ Knew few or no sounds and could not blend at all.
☐ Struggled, but could sound out a few words.
☐ Slowly sounded out many of the words.
☐ Read many of the words accurately and fairly easily.
☐ Read all words accurately and easily.

Notes _____

p. 228, *The Big Collection of Phonics Flipbooks* © 2009 by Lynn Melby Gordon, Scholastic Teaching Resources

Phonics Skill Test 9: *ai, ay*

mail	rain	way	fail
day	gray	jail	play
stain	pay	pain	sail
plain	snail	brain	train

Date:_____

To the parents of _____ .

Phonics Skill Test 9: ai, ay was administered today.

Total words
read correctly

☐ Knew few or no sounds and could not blend at all.
☐ Struggled, but could sound out a few words.
☐ Slowly sounded out many of the words.
☐ Read many of the words accurately and fairly easily.
☐ Read all words accurately and easily.

- -

↟ Give above section to student. ↟

Name _____

Date _____

Total words
read correctly

Skill Test 9: *ai, ay*
Teacher Score Sheet

✓ *Check box if student reads word correctly.*

fail	way	rain	mail
play	jail	gray	day
sail	pain	pay	stain
train	brain	snail	plain

☐ Knew few or no sounds and could not blend at all.
☐ Struggled, but could sound out a few words.
☐ Slowly sounded out many of the words.
☐ Read many of the words accurately and fairly easily.
☐ Read all words accurately and easily.

Notes

Phonics Skill Test 10: *e, ea, ee*

be	sea	meat	real
creek	feet	weak	cheat
wheel	she	three	street
sleep	teach	speed	dream

Date:_____

To the parents of _____ .

Phonics Skill Test 10: e, ea, ee was administered today.

Total words read correctly

☐ Knew few or no sounds and could not blend at all.
☐ Struggled, but could sound out a few words.
☐ Slowly sounded out many of the words.
☐ Read many of the words accurately and fairly easily.
☐ Read all words accurately and easily.

⬆ **Give above section to student.** ⬆

Name_____

Date_____

Skill Test 10: *e, ea, ee*
Teacher Score Sheet

☑ *Check box if student reads word correctly.*

be	sea	meat	real
creek	feet	weak	cheat
wheel	she	three	street
sleep	teach	speed	dream

Total words read correctly

☐ Knew few or no sounds and could not blend at all.
☐ Struggled, but could sound out a few words.
☐ Slowly sounded out many of the words.
☐ Read many of the words accurately and fairly easily.
☐ Read all words accurately and easily.

Notes
_____
_____

p. 230, *The Big Collection of Phonics Flipbooks* © 2009 by Lynn Melby Gordon, Scholastic Teaching Resources

Phonics Skill Test 11: *oa, old, ow*

grow	boat	show	cold
mow	gold	oat	grown
sold	snow	goat	told
blown	mold	crow	throat

Date:_____

To the parents of _____ .

Phonics Skill Test 11: oa, old, ow was administered today.

Total words read correctly

- [ ] Knew few or no sounds and could not blend at all.
- [ ] Struggled, but could sound out a few words.
- [ ] Slowly sounded out many of the words.
- [ ] Read many of the words accurately and fairly easily.
- [ ] Read all words accurately and easily.

↑ **Give above section to student.** ↑ ✂

Name _____

Date _____

Skill Test 11: *oa, old, ow*
Teacher Score Sheet

✓ *Check box if student reads word correctly.*

Total words read correctly

grow	boat	show	cold
mow	gold	oat	grown
sold	snow	goat	told
blown	mold	crow	throat

- [ ] Knew few or no sounds and could not blend at all.
- [ ] Struggled, but could sound out a few words.
- [ ] Slowly sounded out many of the words.
- [ ] Read many of the words accurately and fairly easily.
- [ ] Read all words accurately and easily.

Notes

Phonics Skill Test 12: *ew, oo*

new	boo	cool	look
hoop	chew	droop	pool
too	crew	boot	loop
room	shoot	threw	school

Date:_____

To the parents of _____ .

Phonics Skill Test 12: ew, oo was administered today.

Total words read correctly

☐ Knew few or no sounds and could not blend at all.
☐ Struggled, but could sound out a few words.
☐ Slowly sounded out many of the words.
☐ Read many of the words accurately and fairly easily.
☐ Read all words accurately and easily.

▲ **Give above section to student.** ▲

✄

Name _____

Date _____

Skill Test 12: *ew, oo*
Teacher Score Sheet

☑ *Check box if student reads word correctly.*

new	boo	cool	look
hoop	chew	droop	pool
too	crew	boot	loop
room	shoot	threw	school

Total words read correctly

☐ Knew few or no sounds and could not blend at all.
☐ Struggled, but could sound out a few words.
☐ Slowly sounded out many of the words.
☐ Read many of the words accurately and fairly easily.
☐ Read all words accurately and easily.

Notes

Phonics Skill Test 13: *all, aw*

fall	saw	yawn	tall
lawn	paw	call	fawn
law	all	dawn	draw
mall	drawn	straw	small

Date:_____

To the parents of _____ .

Phonics Skill Test 13: all, aw was administered today.

Total words read correctly

☐ Knew few or no sounds and could not blend at all.
☐ Struggled, but could sound out a few words.
☐ Slowly sounded out many of the words.
☐ Read many of the words accurately and fairly easily.
☐ Read all words accurately and easily.

⬆ Give above section to student. ⬆

✂

Name _____

Date _____

Total words read correctly

Skill Test 13: *all, aw*
Teacher Score Sheet

Check box if student reads word correctly.

fall ☐	saw ☐	yawn ☐	tall ☐
lawn ☐	paw ☐	call ☐	fawn ☐
law ☐	all ☐	dawn ☐	draw ☐
mall ☐	drawn ☐	straw ☐	small ☐

☐ Knew few or no sounds and could not blend at all.
☐ Struggled, but could sound out a few words.
☐ Slowly sounded out many of the words.
☐ Read many of the words accurately and fairly easily.
☐ Read all words accurately and easily.

Notes

Phonics Skill Test 14: *oi, oy*

boy	oil	joy	coil
toy	foil	soy	boil
coy	toil	boy	ploy
spoil	Roy	soil	broil

Date:_____

To the parents of _____.

Phonics Skill Test 14: oi, oy was administered today.

Total words read correctly

- [ ] Knew few or no sounds and could not blend at all.
- [ ] Struggled, but could sound out a few words.
- [ ] Slowly sounded out many of the words.
- [ ] Read many of the words accurately and fairly easily.
- [ ] Read all words accurately and easily.

↑ **Give above section to student.** ↑ ✂

Name _____

Date _____

Total words read correctly

Skill Test 14: *oi, oy*
Teacher Score Sheet

✓ *Check box if student reads word correctly.*

boy	oil	joy	coil
toy	foil	soy	boil
coy	toil	boy	ploy
spoil	Roy	soil	broil

- [ ] Knew few or no sounds and could not blend at all.
- [ ] Struggled, but could sound out a few words.
- [ ] Slowly sounded out many of the words.
- [ ] Read many of the words accurately and fairly easily.
- [ ] Read all words accurately and easily.

Notes

p. 234, *The Big Collection of Phonics Flipbooks* © 2009 by Lynn Melby Gordon, Scholastic Teaching Resources

Phonics Skill Test 15: *ou, ow*

out	how	mouse	howl
sound	town	now	growl
couch	trout	vow	round
cow	found	pouch	clown

Date:_____

To the parents of _____ .

Phonics Skill Test 15: ou, ow was administered today.

Total words read correctly

☐ Knew few or no sounds and could not blend at all.
☐ Struggled, but could sound out a few words.
☐ Slowly sounded out many of the words.
☐ Read many of the words accurately and fairly easily.
☐ Read all words accurately and easily.

↑ **Give above section to student.** ↑ ✂

Name_____

Date_____

Total words read correctly

Skill Test 15: *ou, ow*
Teacher Score Sheet

✓ *Check box if student reads word correctly.*

out ☐	how ☐	mouse ☐	howl ☐
sound ☐	town ☐	now ☐	growl ☐
couch ☐	trout ☐	vow ☐	round ☐
cow ☐	found ☐	pouch ☐	clown ☐

☐ Knew few or no sounds and could not blend at all.
☐ Struggled, but could sound out a few words.
☐ Slowly sounded out many of the words.
☐ Read many of the words accurately and fairly easily.
☐ Read all words accurately and easily.

Notes

Phonics Skill Test 16: *R*-Controlled Vowels

far	sort	dirt	corn
part	fork	dark	more
sport	share	horn	skirt
chair	gear	stork	squirt

Date: _____

To the parents of _____ .

Phonics Skill Test 16: R-Controlled Vowels was administered today.

Total words read correctly

☐ Knew few or no sounds and could not blend at all.
☐ Struggled, but could sound out a few words.
☐ Slowly sounded out many of the words.
☐ Read many of the words accurately and fairly easily.
☐ Read all words accurately and easily.

▲ **Give above section to student.** ▲

Name _____ Date _____

Skill Test 16: *R*-Controlled Vowels
Teacher Score Sheet

✓ *Check box if student reads word correctly.*

far ☐	sort ☐	dirt ☐	corn ☐
part ☐	fork ☐	dark ☐	more ☐
sport ☐	share ☐	horn ☐	skirt ☐
chair ☐	gear ☐	stork ☐	squirt ☐

Total words read correctly

☐ Knew few or no sounds and could not blend at all.
☐ Struggled, but could sound out a few words.
☐ Slowly sounded out many of the words.
☐ Read many of the words accurately and fairly easily.
☐ Read all words accurately and easily.

Notes _____

Phonics Skill Test 17: Consonant Blends

bran	clip	crab	drop
flat	frog	skin	slug
step	spot	trip	glad
quack	skull	split	still

Date:_____

To the parents of _____ .

Phonics Skill Test 17: Consonant Blends was administered today.

Total words read correctly

☐ Knew few or no sounds and could not blend at all.
☐ Struggled, but could sound out a few words.
☐ Slowly sounded out many of the words.
☐ Read many of the words accurately and fairly easily.
☐ Read all words accurately and easily.

- -

↑ **Give above section to student.** ↑

Name _____

Date _____

Total words read correctly

Skill Test 17: Consonant Blends
Teacher Score Sheet

✓ *Check box if student reads word correctly.*

bran	clip	crab	drop
flat	frog	skin	slug
step	spot	trip	glad
quack	skull	split	still

☐ Knew few or no sounds and could not blend at all.
☐ Struggled, but could sound out a few words.
☐ Slowly sounded out many of the words.
☐ Read many of the words accurately and fairly easily.
☐ Read all words accurately and easily.

Notes

p. 237, *The Big Collection of Phonics Flipbooks* © 2009 by Lynn Melby Gordon, Scholastic Teaching Resources

Phonics Skill Test 18: Consonant Digraphs

chat	ship	thin	chop
shut	thick	check	that
thank	which	shock	when
throw	this	thump	throb

Date:_____

To the parents of _____ .

Phonics Skill Test 18: Consonant Digraphs was administered today.

Total words read correctly

- ☐ Knew few or no sounds and could not blend at all.
- ☐ Struggled, but could sound out a few words.
- ☐ Slowly sounded out many of the words.
- ☐ Read many of the words accurately and fairly easily.
- ☐ Read all words accurately and easily.

- ✂

↑ **Give above section to student.** ↑

Name _____

Date _____

Skill Test 18: Consonant Digraphs
Teacher Score Sheet

✓ *Check box if student reads word correctly.*

Total words read correctly

chat	ship	thin	chop
shut	thick	check	that
thank	which	shock	when
throw	this	thump	throb

- ☐ Knew few or no sounds and could not blend at all.
- ☐ Struggled, but could sound out a few words.
- ☐ Slowly sounded out many of the words.
- ☐ Read many of the words accurately and fairly easily.
- ☐ Read all words accurately and easily.

Notes

Phonics Skill Test 19: Prefixes

discover	react	preschool	remove
subway	submarine	unlock	dislike
preview	precook	return	subtest
unzip	refill	unhappy	disinfect

Date:_____

To the parents of _____ .

Phonics Skill Test 19: Prefixes was administered today.

Total words read correctly

☐ Knew few or no sounds and could not blend at all.
☐ Struggled, but could sound out a few words.
☐ Slowly sounded out many of the words.
☐ Read many of the words accurately and fairly easily.
☐ Read all words accurately and easily.

- -

⬆ **Give above section to student.** ⬆ ✂

Name _____

Date _____

Total words read correctly

Skill Test 19: Prefixes
Teacher Score Sheet

✓ *Check box if student reads word correctly.*

discover ☐	react ☐	preschool ☐	remove ☐
subway ☐	submarine ☐	unlock ☐	dislike ☐
preview ☐	precook ☐	return ☐	subtest ☐
unzip ☐	refill ☐	unhappy ☐	disinfect ☐

☐ Knew few or no sounds and could not blend at all.
☐ Struggled, but could sound out a few words.
☐ Slowly sounded out many of the words.
☐ Read many of the words accurately and fairly easily.
☐ Read all words accurately and easily.

Notes _____

Phonics Skill Test 20: Suffixes

calling	pets	painful	yelled
bugs	softly	kicked	shipment
landed	teacher	playful	homeless
quietly	dusty	tested	payment

Date:_____

To the parents of _____ .

Phonics Skill Test 20: Suffixes was administered today.

Total words read correctly

☐ Knew few or no sounds and could not blend at all.

☐ Struggled, but could sound out a few words.

☐ Slowly sounded out many of the words.

☐ Read many of the words accurately and fairly easily.

☐ Read all words accurately and easily.

✂ **Give above section to student.** ✂

Name _____

Date _____

Total words read correctly

Skill Test 20: Suffixes
Teacher Score Sheet

Check box if student reads word correctly. ✓

calling ☐	pets ☐	painful ☐	yelled ☐
bugs ☐	softly ☐	kicked ☐	shipment ☐
landed ☐	teacher ☐	playful ☐	homeless ☐
quietly ☐	dusty ☐	tested ☐	payment ☐

☐ Knew few or no sounds and could not blend at all.

☐ Struggled, but could sound out a few words.

☐ Slowly sounded out many of the words.

☐ Read many of the words accurately and fairly easily.

☐ Read all words accurately and easily.

Notes _____